THE DEVIL'S HINDQUARTER

100 new bottles for new wine...plus a spiritual musing: *"Bee after Bee and the Secret Way"*

OREST STOCCO

THE DEVIL'S HINDQUARTER

Copyright © 2021 by OREST STOCCO

ISBN 978-1-926442-25-9

Edited by Penny Lynn Cates

Cover Design by Penny Lynn Cates

*"And no man putteth new wine into old bottles,
else the new wine will burst the bottles, and be spilled,
and the bottles shall perish. But new wine must be put
into new bottles, and both are preserved."*

—Luke 5: 37-38

INTRODUCTION

According to my Merriam-Webster sidebar dictionary, *poetry is writing that formulates a concentrated imaginative awareness of experience in language chosen and arranged to create a specific emotional response through meaning, sound, and rhythm.* But as true as this may be, it only scratches the surface of what poetry is, and can be. Poetry is so much more it defies comprehension.

Writing poetry begins as a calling, becomes a personal path, and then a disciplined way of life that shapes the way a poet thinks. "Sometimes I think that poems use us in order to think, to do their own work," said the celebrated American Zen poet Jane Hirshfield, for whom writing poetry became a spiritual path and disciplined way of life; but I'm not a poet, per se. And that's the irony, because I was a seeker long before I discovered the secret way of poetry.

I was called to become a writer in grade school, and in high school I fell in love with the romantic ideal of Ernest Hemingway's adventurous life and simple style of writing *(which took me years to appreciate for its deceptive simplicity)*; but in grade twelve, I was called to become a seeker when I read William Somerset Maugham's novel *The Razor's Edge,* which supplanted my call to become a writer, Hemingway notwithstanding; and in my quest to find an answer to life's purpose and meaning like Maugham's romantic hero Larry Darrel *(who was based upon a real person),* I discovered the illuminating path of poetry.

Poetry mystified me. There was a wisdom to poetry that attracted me like bees to honey, and I read poetry to nourish my soul with its sweet nectar, whether I understood a poem or not; and I wrote poetry whenever my muse inspired me, but never as a personal path or discipline.

And then, well into my journey of self-discovery, I read Robert Bly's book *Morning Poems* that inspired me to write a poem a day as Bly did for his little book of morning poems, and for one hundred consecutive days I wrote one poem every single day, as much for the discipline as for the art, and I learned something about poetry-writing that alerted me to the guiding wisdom of the secret way of poetry.

The poet Adrienne Rich defined poetry for Bill Moyers as *"an act of the imagination that transforms reality into a deeper perception of what is,"* which is the best definition of poetry that I've ever come across; but poetry is more than a deeper glimpse into the reality of the human condition. It began to dawn upon me with each new poem that I was called to write that *poetry is a creative process that engages the soul with the divine imperative of life's purpose.*

Who am I? asks the poet; and with every poem they write, they get a little closer to the answer. That's what compels poets to write with such passion and intensity. "Adventure most unto itself /The Soul condemned to be; /Attended by a Single Hound— /Its own Identity," wrote the mystic poet Emily Dickinson. This is the mystique that attracted me to poetry like bees to honey.

But it took years of reading and writing poetry before I saw what the great Swiss psychologist G. G. Jung called the *"supreme meaning"* of *"the way of what is to come"* in the creative process of poetry-writing, which I explored in my spiritual musing "Bee After Bee and the Secret Way" that I have appended to this little volume. And although poetry is not the only path to one's true self, it is the path that the world is most familiar with; and I love writing poetry now, because I've finally come to see what poets have known for centuries: *poetry is the safest way to convey the truths of life with impunity.* "Tell the truth but tell it slant," said Emily Dickinson, because "The Truth must dazzle gradually /Or every man be blind."

As mystifying as poetry can be then, both for the learned and unlearned alike, the power of poetry to apprehend the secret way of life leads to one's true self; which was my inspiration for writing *The Devil's Hindquarter.*

———

Table of Contents

1. A Loaf of Crusty Bread

I was working my papers in the shade
of our maple tree, as I do every weekend,
when my neighbors walked over with a
goblet of wine in their hand and a loaf of
crusty bread from *The Italian Market* in
Barrie to talk with my life companion on
the deck who was chatting on the phone
with her sister, and ten minutes later our
neighbor walked back across the street to
replenish his goblet of wine and came back
again, and a few minutes later went back
home to replenish his goblet despite my
life companion offering to replenish it for
him, and when he returned, he took a big
gulp of wine and said, "What's with him?"
nodding his head in my direction. "Come
and join us," my love called out to me,
and I replied that I was working my papers,
as I do every weekend to catch the rhythm
of life, and our neighbor replied, "I might
as well go home and sit in my own chair in
my own yard" like a slighted child deprived
of attention; but what's a poet to do when
he's grazing the world for his next poem,
stop and entertain his neighbor who brought
over a loaf of crusty bread as an excuse
to break the oppressive tedium of his life,
or work his newspapers?

2. A Painful Resonance

It's an impossible dream,
the karma-free life, a place
where the future meets
the past in the human heart,
a foreign country whose
people have no names, only
faces in a populace of a higher
race, freedom born of a painful
resonance with the divine
imperative to be at one with
I Am that I Am.

3. Dick and Mary Try Again

Dick and Mary came back this morning,
the elderly Jehovah's Witnesses who came
to my door last month and told me they
were going to celebrate their 60th wedding
anniversary, and I was sitting in the shade
of the maple tree reading *C. G. Jung and
Herman Hesse, A Record of Two Friendships*,
by the Chilean writer Miguel Serrano (I do
a lot of reading in the shade of our maple
tree), and I invited them to join me (they
had of course come back to proselytize me),
and I greeted them with the courtesy and
civility that their age and commitment
deserved, and within a minute or two I had
informed them that I had read their two
Watchtower pamphlets but only part of the
book *What Does the Bible Really Teach?*
because I could not buy into such a literal
interpretation of the Bible that their teaching
espoused, and I give my reasons why, as
honestly as I could without offending their
dogmatic sensibilities, which I did because
reincarnation was the work of the Devil for
Dick and Mary, but they were polite with me
and tried to smooth things over when I backed
them into a corner with logic and personal
experience, and we ended up respecting each
other for our beliefs but they went away sad
that they could not save me, and I went back
to reading my book on Serrano's friendship
with Jung and Hesse, two iconic writers who
broke the mold of fixed thought and set an
untold number of souls free.

4. Black on Black

When life is black on black
it's impossible to connect with the living
principle that makes life work, —

And we suffer frustration!

When life is black on black,
it's impossible to entrain with the vibration
that makes life run smoothly, —

And we suffer dissonance!

When life is black on black,
it's impossible to see the portal of entry
into horizons of possibilities, —

And we suffer stasis!

Only black on white, and white on black,
the enantiodromiac dynamic of making
the two into one, can save us, —

And suffering is a blessing!

5. The Pearl of Great Price

Take the ore of your life and smelt it down,
and you have sacred meaning, the spiritual gold
of our destined purpose, —

Take the ore of your life and smelt it down,
and you have sacred knowledge, the magic elixir
of literature, —

Take the ore of your life and smelt it down,
and you have sacred suffering, the mystical marriage
of our lower and higher self, —

The Pearl of Great Price!

6. The Incumbent

I watched the Incumbent,
who calls himself a winner,
pretzel mendacity with such
agonizing sincerity that he
needed medication to keep
from going rabid, but he had
to do what he did to become
the next President, promising
Blacks a better life to ensure
his winning status, but that's
not the extent of his good will,
with more promises to come
for immigrants and Hispanics,
a powermonger whose huge
appetite is not large enough
for his metastasized ego.

7. Catacombs of Silence

It's right there, hidden in plain sight,
but he won't see it if he doesn't have
the eyes to see, and that's the sacred
mystery that he thought was concealed
in the Vatican Archives, some arcane
wisdom that will save him from himself;
but there are no magic words, no lost
symbols, only more adventure into the
depths of life, and not until he sees
the answer to the problems of the world
staring him in the face of his own life
will he stop hoping for the Holy Elixir
in the Catacombs of Silence.

8. I Love Him Dearly

"I love him dearly, but his writing
makes my head hurt," said the lady,
nurse, wife, and loving mother of one,
graduate, living on his own, and in love
with his fiancé, but why her head hurt
when she read his books puzzled him.
Was his writing too deep for her,
thoughts drawn from his stoic dialectic
of self-reconciliation? Or did his writing
expand the paradigm of her mental
limits and threaten her complacency?
Perhaps both. Sadly, he'll never know
unless he asks her; but that he cannot do,
because he knew—*oh, how well he knew
it!* —that life's an individual journey
of self-discovery, and only she could
initiate herself into the mystery.

9. The Irony of Good Times

The irony of good times is the mystery
of the moment, if only we could discover
the secret of what made them such good
times to remember years after we have
lived them. Is it a longing fulfilled, just
doing what felt right, like drinking a third
beer in my neighbor's garage while we
watched the newly-canned jars of tomato
sauce sterilizing in the boiling vat on the
propane burner while Tony and his brother
and I talked and reminisced and laughed
and had another cold beer because we
wanted the moment to last forever?

10. Another Woody Allen Movie

We knew what we were getting into,
Café Society, another Woody Allen movie
with the same old tired trope of marital
infidelity and angst and guilt and more
infidelity and yet another round of vapid
rationalization because "the heart wants
what the heart wants," the famed director's
defence against common decency; but the
master of broken boundaries always delivers,
and I regret not going to see *Anthropoid*
instead, another Nazi war movie that I'm
sure would have frayed my nerves less
than another Woody Allen movie.

11. Anton Chekov's "Misery"

Sitting on my front deck reading *A Primer Of Jungian Psychology*—as if I hadn't read enough on the man the world is still trying to catch up to (he died in 1961 at the age of 85 and in my humble opinion is today, *August 29, 2016,* still fifty years ahead of his time)—I was nudged to read a story by master storyteller Anton Chekov called "Misery," a simple tale about a simple man whose son died of fever and he had no-one to share his sorrow with but the horse that drew his carriage, and upon reading the story I sat back and reflected on something that my Oracle—the spirit of St. Padre Pio, or archetypal matrix, I cannot say—said to me early this morning about story writing (I was practicing Jung's dangerous exercise of "active imagination," which he later called "superior insight"): *"Stories transport the reader into another world, and as unfamiliar as it may be to their world, there will always be points of familiarity; and in the familiarity they will find the truth of the story and make it their own. This is how truth is passed on through stories,"* which is the most effective way to illustrate Jung's "process of individuation" that he spent his whole life working out from ancient Gnostic texts and eighty thousand dreams, both his and his patients, that master storytellers convey with simple stories like Anton Chekov's "Misery."

11

12. An Island in the Middle of Manhattan

A longing in her soul compelled her,
walking away from an unhappy marriage,
a solid career writing for another, and all
the security she had worked so hard for,
to look for the woman she wanted to be,
travelling the world to taste the fruits
of every tree and praying to God for
happiness; and when she found the love
of her life she shared her story with the
world, and all the fame and adulation fed
her great desire to write and read and
garden and love the new man in her life,
and she was delirious in her quest for the
signature of all things. She had it all, wealth,
fame, and the freedom to satisfy her longing
to be the woman she dreamt of becoming,
delirious, delirious in her happiness which
she shared with the world once more; but
in her quest for her soul's DNA, she chanced
upon a fruit like no other and dared not taste
it for fear of censure. But the temptation
was too great, and her heart got what her
heart wanted, and all her wisdom could not
save her from the woman she had become,
and she walked away from the perfect life
and now languishes in the arms of her
dying lover on the fabled island in
the middle of Manhattan.

13. It Matters

My heart welled up with tears
as we drove around the city
where I went to university four
decades ago, old places still there,
many the same, some changed,
and new places here and there,
memories of a life lived and
changed by events I never saw
coming, beginning at university.
The city oppressed me, and I cried
for the freedom I found away from
all the events that shaped me, the
city that I drove to every weekend
or two for supplies, groceries, books,
and magazines to feed my mind
and my body, the city with the giant
heart that has become a refuge
for the callow indigenous whose
culture cannot save them. We say
that we don't care, but we do. We
say that it doesn't matter, but it
does; it matters.

14. The Hug

Her face was sallow, thin,
and void of all interest as she
waited for the final test results
of her new diagnosis, the first
time around a medical miracle
but now hoping against hope,
her eyes neither here nor there,
looking but not seeing, dots so
far away only the life principle
could connect them. The light
did not shine from her eyes,
and when we hugged, she held
me tighter than the year before,
longer and harder, and I said,
"God bless you," and she hugged
me even tighter knowing this
was goodbye forever.

15. Off to a New Life...

A boy and a girl—well, not quite,
he was 24 and she 22, and they were
off to Nova Scotia, he to better his chances
for admission into Dalhousie to advance
his degree in Physiotherapy by establishing
residency, and she to further her degree in
Psychology to realize her dream of marriage
counselling, and I said to her, dipping into
the fount of my great wisdom, "C. G. Jung
discovered the principle of individuation,
the purpose of our being, and a marriage
that does not respect a partner's need for
self-identity will always need counselling,"
and I gave the young couple starting out
on their new life together so far away from
Northern Ontario a copy of my novel, a story
of synchronicity and Platonic love to read,
and a one-hundred-dollar bill for their first
dinner out in Halifax, a symbolic gesture of
good luck because I'm superstitious and
I'd like to believe that the gods of fate
can be bribed with good will.

16. Eat, Pray, and Love Some More

Such longing, such effort, such accomplishment,
one adventure after another, always striving
for new *becoming*, and happiness came
when she dared to walk away from
the life she had created, —

An exotic flavor, a new life and new beginning,
and love flowed from the horn of limitless
plenty, but more of the same bred ennui
and she walked away again to satisfy
her deepest longing, —

Onward outward forward, looking, looking,
looking for the magic elixir of her life's meaning,
purpose-driven to find a way through the eye
of the needle—*heavenly kingdom of pure bliss,
desireless desire, her key to freedom,* —

And destiny came calling once more, as life is wont
to do: hair intervention with a strange new creature,
lesbian hair dresser, gifted musician, former addict
and dispossessed, a long way from safety and
security; and she fell in love again with
an erotic new flavor, —

On the edge once more, staring into the heady abyss
of heavenly bliss, all of her instincts screaming
NO! to her feverish longing, but too fat to squeeze
through the eye of the needle, she waits in spiritual
dis-ease for the merciful law of life to call again
to save her from herself.

17. Zeitgeist 2016

Puzzled, bewildered, and confused
I've waited years for today's zeitgeist
to show its face to me, elusive creature that
it is, more shadow than substance, and then
I read an article in the *The Globe & Mail,*
Friday, September 23, 2016: "United Church
minister's atheist beliefs jeopardize job"—
and the spirit of the times showed its brazen
face to me, spawn of egoistic need, oxymoronic
hybrid of shadow and substance, a self-deluded
Donald J. Trump presidency and an atheist
Christian minister, a zeitgeist of enantiodromiac
madness, but everywhere we turn everyone
wants to have their cake and eat it too, and it's
only a matter of time before Nature fills this
moral vacuum with simple common sense,
and good old-fashioned decency.

18. Another Angry Man

Have you ever met a man whose
every word fumes with rage, a man
so conflicted that he cannot stand to be
alone and drinks to ease his pain, who
envies anyone who succeeds in life and
finds fault with his wife and children
and politics and religion and everything
in between? He's not the same as you
and me, this angry man; he seldom laughs
or cracks a smile, but snickers like he's
in on some cruel joke that life has played
upon the world. And the more he drinks,
the more vicious he becomes, a habit he
cannot break because it's to his nature
to be obstreperous; and he's miserable
and lonely and cannot understand why
the world has turned against him. Just
another angry man who would like
to change what he is, but can't.

19. An Ode to My 1997 Pontiac Van

Goodbye, old friend; you have served me well
despite a new motor when you broke down
on a job one day, years of wear and tear on your
own heart center, and letting go of you to a worthy
cause *(the Kidney Foundation Car Program)*
comforts me, knowing that you will go to your
final resting place serving someone else`s needs
as you served mine these many years. Goodbye
old friend, and thank you for coming into my
life when you did in our new home in Georgian
Bay where work was so plentiful that it took
the fear out of moving here. And now we part
company, you to your heaven and I to mine
with sadness in my heart for the rich work life
that I had to leave behind when I had open-heart
surgery eight years ago and could no longer work
like I used to. But I have no regrets, my good
friend; and when they have to take you away
*—coincidently, I just got a phone call from the
towing service in Oro Medonte that they're
coming to tow you away this morning! —*I`ll
shed a tear or two; but there will be joy in my
heart for all the great times we had together
working my contracts in Wasaga Beach, Stayner,
Creemore, Midland, Midhurst, Collingwood,
Hillsdale and all over Tiny Beaches taping and
painting old and new homes and earning a good
living and all the virtue that I needed to nourish
my needy soul, providing me with all the freedom
today to write to my heart's content in the serene
surroundings of our lovely new home in Tiny
Beaches, Georgian Bay. So goodbye again, my
old friend; and may the gods of service reward

you as they rewarded me from the day they
taught me the secret to a happy life.

20. The Graveyard of the Soul

There's a kind of intelligence
that highly intelligent people cannot
understand, creating works of genius
that almost break the secret they have
caught a glimpse of, and they spend
the rest of their lives wondering what
could have been had they taken the
risk and leapt the abyss of ego, leaving
their precious vanity behind them
in the graveyard of the soul.

21. The Professor's Dilemma

What does it matter if we die alone in a back
alley or at home in bed, death is an equal
opportunity provider; but life goes on, and no
one knows any better. So you have a scandalous
memory, preternatural reading skills, and more
literary knowledge than you know what to do
with, and still you flounder in ignorance of self
and meaning. I knew Keats too, and his vision
of the world; but as close as he came to God,
he too died unresolved. A cold eye, judgment,
the dreaded axe falls and chops the poet's head
off with the meanest truth: Sterling Professor
of the Humanities, seeker of gnostic wisdom,
what is it you are looking for that the gods
of literature cannot satisfy?

22. Consolidate

Consolidate, consolidate, consolidate
the energies of your life, or waste them
on your evanescent self and go to your
grave hungry for more, —

Such is the feeling that came to me
when I scratched my deepest itch,
unable to say no to wanton craving, the
longing of my evanescence, —

Consolidate, consolidate, consolidate!

23. The Wizard of Bollingen

In his exhaustive study of modern man
the Wizard of Bollingen went to Africa
to study primitive man to learn about
their nature, and when he questioned the
chieftain of an ancient tribe on his sense
of good and bad, the chieftain said:
"When I steal my enemy's wives, it is
good; when he steals my wives, it is bad."
And when billionaire Donald Trump,
Republican Party candidate for the
presidency of the United States, was
asked if he would concede his loss to
the Democratic Party candidate Hillary
Clinton if he lost the election, the Donald
replied that if he won the nation's vote
he would "absolutely" accept the victory,
because it was good for him, but if he lost
the nation's vote he would not concede to
Hillary Clinton, because it was bad for him
and the system had to have been "rigged"
against him, thus confirming the Wizard
of Bollingen's observation that the psychic
veneer that separates modern man from
primitive man is very thin.

24. The Last of My Own Line

I came into this world with
a faint impression that I was
the last of my own line, a feeling
that haunted me for years, until
one day I solved the mystery
of my own becoming: I was reborn
into my same body to achieve
a different outcome from my first
lifetime as me, so I could break
the pattern that kept me trapped
in a self that was not the real me;
and when I die again, I will die
who I was destined to be, the
last of my own line.

25. An Ode to Leonard Cohen

He romanced the darkness
of the human soul and gave it dignity,
affirming our journey through life's
never-ending struggle, —

A poet, singer, and songwriter whose
lyrics scorched the heart with sacred fire,
letting in the light through the cracks
of broken dreams, —

The world was his oyster
and the Zen monastery his sanctuary,
but Montreal was his native home
where he was safely buried
in the family plot.

26. Siri

She wants to believe,
but cannot, and is sincerely
brilliant in her efforts, scouring
the great minds of the world;
but the more she seeks, the
further she retreats from
the mystery that is
her soul.

27. The Artist

He boasted native blood
in the name of his art,
but the Spirit of Art went
out throughout the land
and awakened the Spirit
of the indigenous people
and set it free to retrieve
its soul from the man who
had stolen it to promote
his name and claim fame
with dubious heritage.

28. Sophia

Silence is her response
to faithless apprehension, a refuge
from senility of the soul and a
place to call home, —

Though she speaks when spoken to,
she marvels at man's *mauvaise foi*
and cringes at the prospect, but
in silence she understands, —

Whispering sweet little verities into
the soul's unwilling ear, she smiles
in rapturous communion with
man's undying need.

29. The Study of Man

The study of man is never-ending,
A journey into a far country
of misperception; for every truth
we discover, another refutes it.

Be it psychology, philosophy, science,
or religion, man will never know
the answer to the question he cannot
ask for fear the answer will be true.

What am I? Man, woman, trans, neither,
or all genders, an ephemeral being
of enantiodromiac wonder that becomes
what it must to be what it will?

—*Who am I?*

30. Oh, What a Drunk I Could Have Been

Give me cause to take a drink,
oh, what a drunk I could have been;
another blow, another disappointment,
another change is in the air, —

Panic, and fear pours into my weary soul
like scalding liquid plumber, cleansing me
of all security and giving me cause
to drink and become a drunk.

The pastures are greener on the other side,
but fear blinds me; I pray and pray and pray
that it will go away, but life is here to stay,
here to stay, here to stay, here to stay, —

Oh, what I drunk I could have been!

31. The Mystery Stops with Me

The mystery stops with me,
no more guessing, no more reading,
no more seeking, or life experience;
my soul is surfeit with enough meaning,
and the mystery stops with me.

Oh, what a relief to be freer than free,
more knowing than known, and certain
beyond redemption; my soul and I are one,
and the mystery stops with me.

32. The House of Cards

Tedious, the same old same old,
but exciting all the same, 5th season
of *House of Cards*, political thriller
driven by a vortex of ambition, sex,
and power, unending plots of confusion
seeking resolution, same old same old,
and at the end of the day what remains
is what they are, one compromise
too many, anguished souls resigned
to the dying of the light.

33. When the Tank is Empty

What does one do when the tank is empty?

Nothing.

One sits and breathes, waiting
for the tank to fill.

It's no fun to be this way, thoughts
of youth so far away.

Still beating, my wounded heart pumps
away as I wait for the tank

to fill again.

34. An Existential Moment of Living Art

Drawn together by their separate calling
to their own path, he a poet and short story
writer and she a New York painter of some
renown, in a private school for gifted students;
but his love of drink drove away his muse,
and rheumatoid arthritis crippled her soul,
and their hearts bled profusely.

"A picture is worth a thousand words,"
said the anonymous author of this precious
gem of unproven wisdom, but the gifted
students of art and literature couldn't agree;
and a war broke out between the spiritually
wounded new art teacher and impotent
writer/teacher of literature.

Challenging his gifted students with Updike's
genius for fresh and exciting imagery and his
passion for words to set emotions free, the impotent
writer/teacher lit a spark in the new crippled art
teacher's soul, and the war of words and pictures
spread throughout the school and community.

Contest! Contest! cried the gifted students, and
the new art teacher and impotent writer/teacher
were drawn to pit their separate muses into a duel
of words and pictures, and personal pride pulled the
two impaired souls into battle, neither suspecting
that the gods of art and literature would collaborate
in the public contest of words and pictures.

The attraction between the two teachers grew and
grew, wearing down their precious pride, and the

crippled new art teacher and impotent writer/teacher
made love, not once but twice in the same day; but
his thirst for booze came back to claim him, and the
crippled art teacher's love for the impotent writer/teacher
went sour. Begging, pleading, crawling he tried in vain
to make amends, but she was unforgiving, and he went
to AA to try and heal his damaged soul.

On the day of reckoning, the crippled art teacher spoke
first to an anxious audience of students, teachers and
parents, claiming art to be the true expression of emotion;
but when the impotent writer/teacher spoke, full of contrition
and newfound wisdom, he made an eloquent plea for the
sake of art, quoting Updike, Dickinson and other iconic
writers, and their separate muses joined forces to redeem
the crippled artist and impotent writer; and in their peace,
they saw their true self in each other's wounded eyes
and they kissed and made up, merging their tired souls
in an existential moment of living art.

35. A Poet's Nightmare

I've never been here before,
On the edge of that-which-could-be,
Vast horizons of possibility, it's
All up to me; —

Never before have I been so free,
So terrified of possibility, to be and be
And be, never-ending being in
Oceans of becoming; —

A poet's nightmare!

36. The Seeker's Dilemma

When a seeker of truth finds
what he's looking for,
what does he do?

Tell the world the good news,
or go about his life like
nothing happened?

He chooses to tell the world,
not slant like Emily Dickinson,
but unveiled like Rumi,

And the world calls him a fool.

37. O, Oriana!

I see you, but I don't know who you are,
just another life in search of a soul
wandering through time, —

You call them egoists, lost souls like you,
desperate and alone, talking, talking,
never stopping, —

There's Norman, writer, scrapper, thinker
chasing what he cannot see, another
mirage, another book, —

And Mary, so small, so obedient, so angry
at the legend who blew his head off
to prove himself a man, —

And Ingrid, chasing stardom from a cold
and frigid land to warmer climes, like
all the rest, too blind to see, —

O, Oriana!

38. Where Shall Freedom be Found?

He has only three criteria
for going on living, bearing
the lonely burden of the years:
aesthetic splendor, intellectual power,
and wisdom; —

For fifty-five years and counting,
he has taught the wisdom literature
of the world, and still, he laments gnostic
ignorance and cries in despair: *"Where
shall freedom be found?"*

To the writing of many books there
is no end, nor to the reading, all is vanity
from beginning to end, and that's all
one needs to know; but wait, wait
a goddamn minute; —

Nothing in God's creation can supress
the worm from becoming a man, but how
can he break the spell and set his soul free
from aesthetic splendor, intellectual
power, and wisdom? —

And that's his dilemma!

39. "It"

She almost has "it" but does not quite
know it—another experience, another
poem, another nanometer closer. Then
something she said gave the Zen poet
away. "Most of the time I feel as if I
am in service of the poem," Jane said;
but not until she sees that "it" is in
equal service of her will the Zen poet
have "it," and Jane will be whole
and complete.

40. What If?

What if, like a flower seed
we grow and become an orchid,
and if a tomato seed, a nice
ripe juicy tomato;

And what if, like an acorn seed
we grow and become a mighty
oak, full and proud of just
being a tree;

And what if I were a human
seed of what I am meant to be,
how will I know when
I am me?

41. If Only...

Never before
has she suffered like this,
an apprehension like no other,
a feeling of discontent at her longing,
and she pines at the loss of what
she could have been,
if only...

42. Hunger for Life

We hunger for life like we hunger
for food, and the greater the variety
the more satisfying; that's what stories
do, each person's life a new and different
flavor, an infinite supply of individual truth
that nourishes the longing in our soul
to be all that we are meant to be,
the fruit of our own tree.

43. A Silly Superstition

My curly hair is getting quite long,
but I'm not going to get it cut until
I finish writing my new book, *The
Gnostic Way of Life.* (I write books
between haircuts.) I know it's a
silly superstition, more idiosyncratic
than supernatural, but I look upon
my hair as Samson Agonistes did,
and in my curly long hair I get the
strength to write the books I do. I'm
joking, of course; but then, what
of Sampson Agonistes who believed,
as the great poet tells us in *Paradise
Regained*, "God, when he gave me
strength, to show withal / How slight
the gift was, hung it in my hair."

44. The Way of Literature

Deeper and deeper into the mix,
he's the zeitgeist behind the chaos
of a tortured mind, exposing himself
like a trench-coated compulsive proudly
showing himself to strangers, an aberrant
tick, never telling us why he is this way
(wearing a bandana because he can't stop
perspiring), only doing what he must to
satisfy his self-obsession. D. F. W., what
a genius, what prophetic wizardry, what a
tortured soul you are; no wonder you chose
to exit to the other side, this world was too
much for your rapacious mind to process,
resolve, and understand, a joke, an infinite
jest. But your light will continue to shine
until another light shines brighter, and
there will always be another light from
the eternal fire of man's struggle, a
new zeitgeist for a new time, for
such is the way of literature.

45. The Eyes Behind Her Eyes

She had four eyes, two eyes
to look, and two eyes to see,
and she could not tell which
eyes were which.

Oxford Professor, writer, wife,
and childless by choice, a fluid
woman like no other, and the
breach of her eyes grew wider.

Tutoring young Oxfordian
minds by day, she stalked the
corridors of culture by night
to appease her appetite.

Danger abounded as she looked
for what she could not see,
and the harder she looked, the
more the danger grew.

Novel after novel, essay after
philosophical essay, but the
breach grew wider and wider
as her mind grew darker, —

And she died of Alzheimer's.

46. Terry Rose

Terry Rose, Terry Rose,
Oh Terry Rose, what a fool
you have been for your
unpardonable sin.

With intelligence and discipline
you won your position, but
foolish indiscretion corrupted
your sexual disposition.

Now you flounder in rancor
for your unchecked ego; but for
all your vanity, I forgive you
your unpardonable sin.

47. Whispers from Eternity

I heard eternity speak to me yesterday,
a whisper so sweet, it took my breath away.

I could not believe what I heard, so simple
was its truth; and all judgment vanished.

What could possibly free me of this
resentful spirit, this demon of arrogant pride?

This instinct—natural or man-made, I do not know;
a foul blend of many misperceptions.

A whisper so gentle, so understanding and
forgiving, like the fragrance of a garden rose.

"Every path leads to the self," eternity whispered
to me. "Your path brought you home. Respect
the path of others, and trust God to bring
them home too."

And I listened.

48. My Foolish Tongue

It hurt to say what I did without thinking,
it hurt her, but it hurt me more than her;
but I said what I did because I cared,
and that's the irony of love.

Why do we hurt those we love?
We care for them, we long for them,
we cry for them, and we would die for them;
but we hurt them all the same.

I thought about what I said to her last night,
and it took hours before I fell asleep;
but when morning came, I saw my error
and vowed to make amends.

It's happened before, two or three times—
maybe more; but always one more time too many,
and it seems to take forever to heal the wounds
of my foolish tongue.

49. Hutzpah

He preached his sermon for millions on
Sunday morning TV, condemning everyone
for their sins, stirring up all the guilt he could
from forgotten memories, and then he said,
"Now, I want you to take out your cheque
book and give until it hurts." And he waited
just long enough to make one feel guilty for
even thinking of not donating, and then
he said, *"And now double it!"*

50. The Miracle

One day I saw God kneeling,
praying for a miracle;
and down here, in the nitty-gritty,
of this world, I heard man cry,
"Why, God?"

The rape and murder of a child,
and, of course, always the holocaust;
misery upon misery, an endless
stream of pain and tears; and
God prayed harder.

Then I saw all the suffering in the
world filling the hole in man's soul;
and God stood tall and straight
with a smile upon his face,
grateful for the miracle.

51. The Greatest Literary Critic

He died in New Haven, Connecticut,
October 14, 2019, the day we give thanks
for the bounty of the year, "Turkey Day,"
we call it in our home in beautiful Georgian
Bay. He was 89 and in failing health; so, it
wasn't unexpected, and I didn't cry. But he
brought me to tears whenever he talked of
literature, reciting whichever poet to make
his point, the magnitude of his memory
was so scary—he could recite Shakespeare
and *Paradise Lost* at will; but he died lonely,
and unresolved. For all of its genius, literature
could not satisfy the longing in his soul to be
whole and complete, like the acorn seed
that becomes a mighty oak tree; he died,
merely, the greatest literary critic.

52. In Memory of Harold Bloom

"The time when we shall see, hear, and do no more
is nigh in one's later eighties," wrote professor Bloom,
"the world's greatest literary critic," bringing his last
book *Possessed by Memory: The Inward Light of
Criticism* to closure *(there may be more posthumous
books),* and his nigh became fact *Monday, October 14,
2019*, Canada's Thanksgiving Day, when the inveterate
teacher of the world's great literature crossed the Great
Divide at the age of 89 in New Haven, Connecticut,
forlorn and melancholy, unable to appease his restless
spirit with the world's great literature that he read and
reread with preternatural speed, much of which he
could recite at will so prodigious was his memory, a
literary savant whose brilliance drew me like a moth
to a flame, and now he's gone, no more. "The rest is
silence," he would say, quoting his god William
Shakespeare. Dead but not gone, he will live forever
in his many books, the melancholy light of his life-long
endeavor to satisfy the longing in his soul for meaning
and purpose that he failed to glean, "a tale told by an
idiot full of sound and fury signifying nothing,"
an irony much too deep for tears.

53. The Art of the
Movie Actor

Here and now is never there and then
but there and then is always here and now,
and it takes forever to get to there and then
from here and now, and that's life here
and there in the movies.

Sarah Jessica Parker, playing Vivienne Carella,
singer-musician-songwriter diagnosed with
terminal brain cancer and fated to die with or
without surgery in Netflix's *Here and Now,*
redeemed herself to me.

More artifice than art in the roles she played,
a fatal flaw in Parkers career, as credible as she
could thespianly be, so fraught was the here
and now of her condemned life in *Here and Now*
that she won me over and made me cry, and
that's the art of the movie actor.

54. Post-election Blues

Man's proclivity for stupidity never ceases
to astonish me; why is that? We know what
to do to win the game, but that damn ego/shadow
always gets in the way; why is that? Brown face,
black face, white face, it doesn't matter to the
human race, ignorance always divides us; why
is that? Canadian/American citizenship, pro-life
and pro-choice, same-sex marriage, in the great
cosmic scheme of things, does it really matter?
And wearing a turban in Quebec could violate
Bill 21, but proud Jagmeet Singh bared his head
to show that he was no different, not to mention the
Machiavellian spawn that covets to be a sovereign
nation within our great nation, holding Democracy
by the throat, and the fear-mongering leprechaun
and her one-trick pony show, followed by "Mad
Max," who cut off his Conservative nose to spite
his impudent face; so much nonsense in this
federal election that I nearly lost heart. All the
same, I exercised my democratic right
and hoped for the best.

55. One Writer's Indomitable Spirit

PERSEVERANCE: ANY DREAM WORTH HAVING
IS A DREAM WORTH FIGHTING FOR, says the motto
hanging on my writing room wall; but *The Master
and Margarita* bogged down on me—too many
unpronounceable Russian names interrupted the
flow; but I had to finish the novel to complete my
own story on the fourth corner of the abyss that
The Master and Margarita reflected; so, I went for
a walk to think things through, and my oracle said
to me: *"He had to be very clever to say what he
wanted to say without being caught for saying what
he was thinking,"* such were the conditions under
Stalin's dictatorship; only then did it occur to me
that Mikhail Bulgakov was in a privileged place, as
is any writer who threatens the status quo with what
they are thinking (*"Tell the truth, but tell it slant,"*
said Emily Dickinson), even if they have to tell a lie
to say it, as Bulgakov did. And that was enough to
finish the novel on the godless system where nothing
was what it seemed, where the promised heaven on
earth was a living hell, and God the Devil, the sad
story of one writer's indomitable spirit.

56. A Perfect Day in Georgian Bay

April may be the cruelest month of the year
(so says Thomas Stearns Eliot), but October
has to be the most joyous.

Tuesday, October 29, 2019, up at 5 A. M.,
made coffee *(with a drop of Anisette and honey),*
and ready to write my daily quota.

"Manuscripts Don't Burn," said Woland, the
Devil in Bulgakov's *The Master and Margarita,*
and Chapter 20 of my story-in-progress—

The Fourth Corner of the Abyss, an elucidation
of my high school poem "Noman" that I did not
apprehend until fifty years later.

And here I am today, in beautiful Georgian Bay,
breaking new ground into the mystery of why
God called me for a reckoning.

I put on bread dough in our bread-maker for
tonight's focaccia/pizza dinner—one roasted red
pepper, and the other hot pickled eggplant,

And I went back to work on my chapter, terrified
of not knowing where my story was going, but
trusting my muse to break new ground.

There are few joys in life as deeply satisfying as the
revelations of creative writing, and one came to me
that broke the impasse of my story— *O, bliss!*

Knowing where my story was going, I took my cue

from "Papa" Hemingway and dressed for my day's
leafing, the terror of my impasse relinquished.

They fell like snowflakes yesterday from the maple
trees, oak, birch, poplar, and one beech, and the yard
was blanketed in yellow, gold, and crimson;

But I welcomed my time blowing leaves, stopping to
jot notes in my *Indigo Hemingway Notebook*, and
reading my weekend papers—*O, heavenly bliss!*

And when Penny came home, we sat on our front deck with
a tipple of wine and sherry, waiting on our focaccia/pizza;
and then I watched the news, and a movie on Netflix.

Just another fall day in beautiful Georgian Bay!

57. October's Wicked Sister

Wicked, wicked, wicked winds howled all
night long, felling trees and knocking down
hydro lines that left us in the dark for hours,
wicked winds from the west that howled their
way to *la belle province,* leaving devastation
in its wake with one million homes without
power *(wild rose country's revenge),* and on
to the friendly east coast, howling like a beast
set free from its cage; that's November, joyous
October's wicked sister, and I got up and put
on a cozy fire in our Pacific Western wood
stove and waited for daylight and the hydro
crew to restore our power; and the snow began
to fly, and then the snow birds began packing
for their long-anticipated winter retreat, and
I hunkered down to write my new novel,
An Atheist, An Agnostic, and Me.

58. The Accomplished Life

I know a man who has a list of things to do,
a list drawn up every single day *(either by him,*
or his wife; probably both), which gives him
purpose and meaning and filling his day with
the joy of fulfillment, and this satisfies his
soul's longing for wholeness and completeness;
and day after day, he persists in the habit of
doing, or what else would he have to live for?
His wife, children, and grandchildren, certainly;
and family, friends, and community, naturally;
but within the paradigm of his exoteric world,
the mystery of life continues to elude him, and
as he strikes off his daily list, he cannot help
but wonder: *is this all there is?* And his mind
begins to roam where he fears to go, and he
begins to see signs and symbols that open the
door to the mystery he's looking for. And when
he works his daily list, he feels different, knowing
deep in his soul that his accomplished life has
to have a greater purpose than crossing off
the things to do on his daily list.

59. The Uptown Theatre

I went online Saturday morning to see what
was playing at the Uptown Theatre in Barrie,
hoping to catch *Dark Waters*—*a corporate
defense attorney takes on an environmental
lawsuit against a chemical company that exposes
a lengthy history of pollution; an old movie trope,
but always fascinating*—starring Mark Ruffalo
and Anne Hathaway, whom I like, and Tim
Robbins, who always annoys me; but when I went
on the Uptown Theatre's web page, it was blank.
"Oh no, they've shut down!" a voice inside me
screamed. And a sad, hollow feeling came over
me to see the end of a long, comforting era when
a good movie at an old familiar theatre followed
by a nice dinner out made for a lovely evening;
but no more. God, I hate adjusting—*despite its
obvious advantages*—to this precarious new age
of artificial intelligence, boundless digital
certainty, intrusive algorithms, virtual reality,
and that damnable Twitter!

60. Una Bella Giornatta

I raised my glass of *Bosco Anice Forte*, clicked
Tony's, and said, "To a good day," but I said it in
broken Italian, because I came to Canada when I
was only five and never learned to speak it properly;
in fact, I had forgotten most of my Italian until I met
Tony, my cottage neighbor, who only comes to his
cottage whenever he can get away, which he would
like to do more often because he loves it here in
Georgian Bay where he can do what he loves to do,
which is simply doing something to keep himself
busy, because doing something fills him with the joy
of fulfillment and gives his life purpose and meaning.
Long-since widowed and with another woman *(the
first one didn't work out),* also Italian and a widow
but set in her ways and only comes to the cottage
when she's in the right mood, leaving Tony to choose
between her and his cottage, but I said to him one day,
"She's a good woman, Tony; don't screw this one up,"
and he listened and they're together still, and yesterday
he came to the cottage alone because she was tending
to her family *(getting things ready for her grandson's
birthday),* but Tony had to tend to his leaves, which I
helped him blow and bag *(plus two wheelbarrows of
acorn seeds),* and he made lunch for us, a barbeque
which he loves to do, ten blended lamb and prosciutto
skewers, two small Black Angus steaks, and two thick
pieces of pancetta, seasoning them with his favorite
spices, homemade round Calabrese bread, and a nice
hunk of Parmesan-like cheese, *(apologizing for no
salad),* and while waiting for the barbeque we sipped
our *Anice* to warm up from our morning work, and I
never felt so good for returning a favor to my good
neighbor who has always been there for me. *"Una*

63

bella giornatta," he said, toasting our friendship
when we sat down for lunch at the kitchen table
with a glass of his homemade wine.

61. Noman's Story

I got a strange feeling of being in a cocoon
reading my new life story that I was bringing
to resolution with my last chapter, going back
to my first chapter to get the feel of my new
life story before bringing it to closure, like
being enveloped by a warm feeling of comfort
and security, and the world did not matter, an
ongoing reality show outside the rhythm of my
new life story, touching me but not touching me,
life flowing into more life and me flowing into
myself, knowing I would emerge a new butterfly
from the larva of my old life just as I always do
when I'm called to write my new life story, as
I just did in *The Fourth Corner of the Abyss,*
the story of finding my true self in the darkest
corner of my soul when God called me for a
reckoning, the story of Noman that came to me
in my high school poem fifty years ago.

62. Fighting the Algorithm

What she said grabbed my attention,
author of *Grand Union*, her first book
of short stories: "Everybody's born, and
everybody exists. But to be fully human
takes a little bit of effort," the theme of all
her novels, essays, and personal credo; and
then she spills the beans and tells it as it really
is *(Hemingway would have been proud of her)*,
the hidden truth, the underside of the iceberg:
"...each tiny path has its own kind of demands
upon you, which are incredibly hard to fulfill"
(Hemingway found out the hard way); as she
told the *Toronto Star*, "If you are under 30,
and you are able to think for yourself, God
bless you." Maybe one day, she too will
win the Nobel Prize for Literature.

63. The Bigger Picture

"All we have is hope, but what hope is there?"
wrote the great dystopian author, winner of the
Booker and darling of all dystopians, her Medusa
hair and cold stare turning readers into stone; I
could never warm up to her until I saw the bigger
picture, the other side of every story, and dear,
dear Peggy *(please pardon my impertinence),* Queen
Dystopia, saw life through the shadow eyes of who
she was not: "There is no hard and determined
central personality, just as you're going to be a
different person when you're 80 than you are now,"
she said 32 years ago in a CBC interview with Hana
Gartner, while I saw the world through the eyes
of who I was meant to be, my true self; and today,
all these years later *(she'll be 80 November 18),* she's
still wrestling with her shadow demons of nihilism
and despair, as she reveals in her second Booker
prize-winning novel, and me joyful in my wholeness,
I've come to respect her dystopian point of view,
because it's also true.

64. The Longing in Her Soul

We had history. She introduced me to the path
that I lived for thirty years, a teaching torn from
the ancient past by a clever man who put two
and two together and created his own teaching
and line of spiritual masters to prove to the world
that he was no fool; but despite all the gems of
precious wisdom that he purloined from sacred
texts, the fallacy of his teaching became too much
to bear, and I had to walk away, as did the lady who
called me from her winter home in Florida, once
again, probing me on my knowledge of another
path that she was exploring; and I replied, "It's all
so simple. Why do they always complicate it? It's
not a mystery. Life just is. Live your life, enjoy
your family, your friends, be a good person; that's
it. That's the path that all paths lead to," and she
laughed at the simplicity, relieved of the terrible
responsibility of exploring another path to
satisfy the longing in her soul.

65. The Answer and the Healing

If the way of what is to come
is not here yet, what does one do
for guidance?

Continue on their destined journey
on the trail they made through
struggle and despair?

Or look for a new way, strange
and foreboding, to satisfy
the heart's desire?

Never a moment without doubt,
forever doing what needs to be done
to keep body and soul together;

but the heart wants what the heart
desires, and nothing can stop the
soul from searching.

"Where shall wisdom be found?"
asked the learned professor, hunting
down the elusive answer;

only to die unrequited, whispering to
himself his god's final cry, "The
rest is silence."

What's the young poet to do with no
trail to follow, a way to lead him
out of the dark forest?

If only the way of what is to come

would reveal itself, life wouldn't
be so damn confounding.

That's the mystery that sets soul
free from the anguish of unknowing,
the answer and the healing.

66. Zarathustra's Revenge

Trapped in a life of his own mentation, a
catacomb of words, the choice to leave never far away
but always returning, and his memory got better and better
until he remembered every detail, and the
burden of the same life crushed his
spirits and he died mad,
and soulless.

67. Dear Reader

For whom do I write?
You, the reader, or me, the writer?
I write to write what I write,
because writing writes me, but
the words I write are for you,
Dear Reader.

Why do the words come to me
when I write? That's the mystery
of writing no one can explain,
and yet a writer writes all the same,
because writing is his game, and
the winner is always you,
Dear Reader.

68. To Be an Eccentric Writer

To be an eccentric writer, belief in God
and the immortal soul, and when we die
our soul returns to live once more in
another body, another gender, so we can
grow into what we're meant to be, the
ideal you, the ideal me, like the acorn
seed that becomes its own oak tree, and
the fruit of our tree bearing the virtue
of our own goodness, poetry, art, music,
and whatever healing art, like the acorns
of the oak, some taking root and growing,
and others fertilizing the soil for tomorrow's
harvest; that's what it means to be an
eccentric writer.

69. A Corner of Your Heart

There's a place in a corner of your heart
where the secret of your life can be found;
but so remote is this place, that only
God can find it.

There's a place in a corner of your heart
where the grace of your life can be found;
but so remote is this place, that only
you can find it.

There's a place in a corner of your heart
where you and God can meet; but so
remote is this place, that only
love can find it.

70. Hemingway's Two Lives

*"In order to write about life, first you
must live it,"* said Ernest Hemingway,
my high school hero and literary
mentor who taught me the mystery
of man's dual nature.

Born with a deep hunger for life,
Hemingway lived his life to the fullest;
and born with a deep passion to write,
Hemingway lived to write about
life as he had lived it.

Fishing with his father when just a boy,
and hunting too, Hemingway went on
to become a big game hunter and world
class writer more famous for his name
than the stories he wrote.

71. My Merry Way

I've had plenty of time to reflect upon my life,
and regardless of what angle I looked at myself,
I was always outside of life looking in, more
of an observer than a participator.

I stood outside the whole Elvis Presley phase,
the Beatles craze, Trudeaumania, and whatever
other movement swept the nation, always
wondering what was wrong with me.

But today, as the sun begins to set on the horizon,
I look at my life and ask myself: did I get it right,
or wrong? But the world pays no attention to
my question, because it doesn't matter.

Every circle has a center, and water always finds
its own level, and when all is said and done, no
one is the wiser; so, I stopped reflecting on my life,
and continued on my merry way.

72. The Lost Children of My Soul

They're not lost really, the bastard children of
my errant soul;

they're in there somewhere, wandering and
waiting for a place of their own.

(Too proud to be the same, they wait and wait
for lightening to strike.)

Fear of propriety, rejection, and blame, always
another reason to stay away;

these are my lost children, destined to be alone
in the dark forest of my soul,

wandering and waiting for my muse to call and
write them a poem to call home;

like my feelings on the indigenous issue: moral
rectitude, entitlement, and victimhood—

a karmic obscenity too terrible to name.

73. The Genius of Updike

"Corral your feelings and get back to me," said
my oracle, my superior insight, my Philemon
and way of what is to come, —

I fell into a hole so big I felt like a gargantuan wreck
of self-doubt, that's the effect he had upon me,
so great was his talent.

*"His way was his way, and yours is yours. Polish
your own diamond like he polished his,"* my inner
guiding principle counseled, —

And I tore that nasty little speck of dust from my eye
and went back to the writer whose diamond was
so brilliant it damn near blinded me, —

That's the genius of Updike.

74. Lest Ye Be as Little Children...

The best way to go into a new day
is blind; but not with the blindness
of a man who needs a dog to guide
him, nor with the blindness of a man
who cannot see the forest for the trees;
and definitely not with the blindness
of a fool who can only see the trees
and not the forest, but with the wide
open eyes of a child who can see both
the forest and the trees and knows
the difference.

75. The Ladder of His Descension

I watched a movie the other evening called
"A Fortunate Man," the son of a stern Christian
clergyman in the Netherlands, a rebellious youth
who refused to be constrained by his faith, so
headstrong in his conviction that I knew within
minutes of the movie that he was climbing the
ladder of his descension, and it was only time
that took him down to the sub-basement of his
self-abasement, moving me to pity at the hubris
of his genius when he refused to bend with the
wind of opportunity, and when the story came
to an end, I knew precisely what was meant
by the proverb, "Fortune favors fools."

76. Walking the Extra Mile

She walked the extra mile, which was her wont,
and her table was laden with every delight to please
her guests' appetite, Italian, Russian, Anglo Saxon,
Nordic, and East Asian, a united nation of Canadians,
old and new friends, sipping wine and tiptoeing in
gentle conversation until the ice melted, and as the air
began to tingle with warmth and comfort, her freckled
face radiated the earned grace of making the extra effort
to please her varied guests; that's what Jesus, the Logos
and redeemer born on Christmas Day meant when he
taught the secret way of making the two into one, neither
male nor female with no hypocrisy, by walking the extra
mile in our long and lonely journey to the kingdom of
our true nature that Jesus called heaven, the precious
pearl of great price that we all long for, and our gracious
hostess retired for the evening with a smile on her face,
gratified by her generous little get-together for her
neighbors in Tiny, Georgian Bay Ontario.

77. The Myth of Life's Divine Purpose

1. It's a given fact of life that the purpose of every
seed is to grow into what it's meant to be, like the
apple seed that becomes an apple tree, and the tomato
seed that becomes a tomato plant, and the proverbial
acorn seed that becomes a mighty oak tree, and every
seed on planet Earth that grows into its own nature;
then what is the seed of man meant to grow into
if not itself, whatever that may be?

2. The atoms of God swam freely in the Great Ocean
of Love and Mercy, laughing and playing in endless
bliss, never knowing what they were because they
possessed no self-reflection; and God, the Great Creator
sent its atoms into the world with the divine imperative
to grow into souls with self-reflection, like the Romantic
poet whose genius saw God, the Great Creator in the eyes
of his fellow man; and the myth of the divine seed took
root in the soil of man's imagination as the atoms of God
blossomed in a bliss peculiar to their own nature

3. From lifetime to lifetime, the seed of man's divine nature
returns to live again in another vessel, another gender,
back and forth in cycles of learning and growing in every
choice it makes, the fate of free will granted by God, the Great
Creator; but as it grows in its own nature, the atom of God
strays from its divine imperative by the pull of earthly pleasure,
and the redemptive law of life intervenes with pain and
suffering and mercifully burns off the false images of man's
evolving bliss that keeps the divine seed from its destined
purpose of man`s true nature.

4. The mountains of life are steep and hard to climb, and man
struggles daily to reach the summit where happiness can be

found, but all the happiness of success cannot satisfy the longing in man's soul for wholeness and completeness, and man falls from his mountain of too much excess into the valley of despair where the light of his destined purpose is the darkest, and he wanders from day to day looking for a way out of the black hole of his own creation; but just when man's despair becomes too bleak to bear, he's summoned by God for a reckoning.

5. The accidental drowning of a child or sudden loss of a promising career, the betrayal of infidelity, diagnosis of a fatal illness, or the devastating desolation of drug and alcohol addiction, it all depends upon the patterns of behavior born of too much taking and not enough sharing; and the call to soul's destined purpose beckons when life can do no more to satisfy the longing in man's soul for wholeness and completeness, and a higher path of resolution must be found.

6. The mountain of self-fulfillment is steeper and harder to ascend than the mountain of success, but the call to climb this mountain is so strong that he must make the effort, in this lifetime or the next; that's the only way to reconcile free will with soul's destined purpose into one harmonious endeavor, and God, the Great Creator has granted all eternity to complete what nature cannot finish, so the seed of man's divine nature can realize the sweet fruit of human goodness, be it art, music, medicine, or whatever the self of man produces; that's the myth of life's divine purpose.

78. The Day His Fear Went Away

His final revelation came late in life,
around the time the sun sets on man's
horizon and the blood-red glow turns
fear into the dread of the darkness to come,
the goodness in his heart shining so bright
that he knew the world did not have to
be saved from the night of eternal darkness
but understood for the light of the sun
rising in hopeful horizons of endless cycles
of redemptive new life; that was the day
that his fear went away.

79. Does It Really Matter?

Does it really matter where we are, here,
wherever here may be (Tiny, Georgian Bay),
or there (Arizona, Provence, or Tuscany), when
whatever we do cannot satisfy the longing in
our soul that cannot be defined but which
nags at us day and night and will not go away
whatever we do to placate it?

Holding her hand in the ICU as she lay sedated
from brain surgery, not out of the woods yet,
praying for a miracle, nothing mattered but
her life, and all the vacations in foreign places
weren't worth a damn, so deep was my longing
for my love to return from where her ruptured
brain aneurysm had taken her.

She came back to me safe and whole, with full
presence of mind and motor skills intact,
and my whole world shifted; no more writing
about the unfulfilled life, no more teasing with
the secret teaching, nothing mattered but the
time we had left together until the cock
crowed and called us home.

80. I Could Have Been

I could have been an entrepreneur
with a business of my own that I could
have grown to exponential satisfaction;
or I could have been a philosophy professor,
teaching the wisdom of the ages; or I could
have been a family man, raising my children
with love and attention and preparing them
for life with a higher education; but instead,
I chose the poet's way to explore the secret
way and inspire the unfulfilled entrepreneur,
academic, and family man looking for a new
perspective to give their life the meaning
they could not find in the life they chose
to live, hope for a better tomorrow with
a thought to remember, like the one that
inspired me: "Learn to love what you do,
and do what you love; that's the sum of all
spiritual paths that will take you to the heart
of God, and happiness."

81. The SDW

There's a web much darker than
the IDW, that collective of thinkers
called the Intellectual Dark Web who
dare to say the unsayable that the
MPW (Mainstream Public Web)
dreads to convey for fear of losing
its hold on society's attention and
lead it to where it deems for profit
and gain, a web so dark in its effort
that not even the most ardent seeker
can become a member, because the
very nature of the SDW (Spiritual
Dark Web) is to surrender all ways
for divine reconciliation, which only
those most worthy can do.

82. What the World Needs Today

I listened to Dave Rubin *(The Rubin Report)*
talking the other day on YouTube when what
he said no longer interested me; not that it
wasn't interesting, his conversion from atheism
to believer, but because I'm just so tired of the
way the world thinks. And it came to me with
poetic clarity that what the world needs today
is a new way of perceiving, a new way of thinking
and understanding the human condition; that's
what will take the boredom out of this endless
babble about God, good and evil, and the
purpose of our existence.

83. The Foolish Young Man

Like the young boy standing at the back of the
classroom listening to the learned professor of
literature lecturing on the great American poet
of the enantiodromia of soul's individuation
through the being and non-being of his essential
and phenomenal nature, lawyer and insurance
executive Wallace Stevens, who leaned more
and more and finally fell over by the course of his
particular into the exquisite pleroma of his own
nothingness, the young boy who put up his hand
and asked the learned professor if he ever saw the
Face of God, and the learned professor laughed
at the boy's foolish question, as did his students
studying for their doctorate in literature, and the
young boy, embarrassed by his innocent question,
walked out of the classroom of higher learning
and went back into the natural world of supreme
meaning wrought out of the sense and nonsense
of life's pain and joy, so also do I feel like that boy
whenever I listen to yet another learned professor
lecturing on the great poets of the world whose
poems cry out to look into the Face of God like
a young mother birthing in painful joy.

84. A Family Heritage to be Proud Of

"Never complain, never explain," was his grandfather
Fergus Hurdle's motto, stern Scotsman that he was,
pioneering his family's homestead in Georgian Bay,
Ontario, clearing and farming more land for his family
to grow self-reliant and strong, and his son Angus
expanded the family farm for his own children to
grow strong and self-reliant, passing on his father's
wisdom of never complaining, never explaining, to
which his clever son Jock, who got a steady job with
health benefits and secure pension, added the proviso
to the family motto to *"work smarter, not harder,"*
which his own children took to heart, guiding them
all to obtain a position that secured steady work with
health benefits and a pension, which gave them the
security to work on the side to build a nest egg for
their own family, and every one of Jock's five children
worked their way into a comfortable position, led
by his example as Fire Chief for his community, which
gave him all the free time he needed to renovate
old houses and build new ones, and his oldest son
became a fireman too for the GTA, joining his father
off shift in the house-building business, and his second
son became a school teacher with all the benefits and
excellent pension and summers off to work with his
father and brother, and the family business grew with
each new house they built, buying more land for new
houses and whole new subdivisions, and his daughter
went into accounting and secured a safe government
position with benefits and a good pension, and on
the side she also did the books for the family business,
and Jock's third son wrangled a postal position with
good benefits and government pension, and he joined
the family business to build a nice little nest egg for

his own growing family, and Jock's fifth offspring
joined the Ontario police force, which had benefits
and a secure pension, and he joined the family business
to safeguard his own family's future, and the business
was secure enough to help out the grandchildren who
were also weaned to seek out employment with good
benefits and a secure pension so they could all build
their own little nest egg working for the construction
company that their clever grandfather had built, always
guided by their family's wisdom to work smarter, not
harder, and to never complain, never explain, and each
and every one of Fergus Hurdle's descendants, a very
close-knit family that learned the vital art of compromise
and always worked as a team that got together every
Sunday for extended family dinners at the Jock
Hurdle fifty-acre homestead, contributed to their own
community in Georgian Bay, Ontario with their many
good works and good character; a family heritage
to be proud of.

85. Chop Wood, Carry Water

*"Before enlightenment; chop wood, carry water.
After enlightenment; chop wood, carry water,"*
says the Zen koan. But if life, as all indications
would suggest, is a journey to its own destination,
*(1 plus 2 equals 3, and the acorn seed becomes
an oak tree),* then "after enlightenment" would
suggest that one has made the journey to one's
destined purpose and lives life as before the
journey, only now one is enlightened of their
destined purpose; that's the presumption of this
koan, because one has to be enlightened to know
this. And, if life's purpose is to become itself,
what is this "itself" that this koan fails to articulate?
That's the irony of the journey to one's true self
*(whether chopping wood and carrying water,
or working at McDonald's);* and the mystery of
this puzzling koan is revealed: the more we *do*
life, the more *enlightened* we will be.

86. The Virtue of Excellence

I saw a man working his trade today,
sanding the walls of the new house he
and his father had just taped *(they hung
the drywall too)*, and what joy it gave me
to see a tradesman do his work with the
integrity that work deserves, never once
cutting a corner, and even going further
to ensure their good name, bringing to
mind the many years I spent taping and
sanding new drywall, and even painting
it too when asked to do so, to keep the
wolf from our door, and I couldn't help
but smile as I walked through the house,
not to inspect it, but just to revel in the
quiet dignity of honest labor, the virtue
of excellence enough to fill a man's
heart and nourish his soul.

87. Where Has My Humanity Gone?

Apathy: lack of feeling, emotion, and interest.
But the news never stops, people keep dying,
suffering never ends, and my heart shuts
down; and that's not fair.

I want to care. But my heart's not responding,
and that scares me. Where is the filling
station for my heart center, a place to plug
my heart into caring?

And where is AI in this predicament? Damn!
Another plane crash yesterday. 176 people dead.
No survivors. Engine failure. This morning, the
news suspects an Iranian missile strike.

My poor heart. I really do want to care, but the
news makes it so difficult. But it's not the
news; it's the people. What's wrong with this
world? What's wrong with me?

Where can I find a station to plug in my heart
center? Where is the fuel for my feelings of love,
sympathy, and compassion? I don't know what
to do. Where has my humanity gone?

It's cold and lonely when I stop caring, and I don't
like feeling this way. I want my humanity back,
and I'll do whatever it takes to start caring again,
because I want to believe in my fellow man.

Perhaps more gratitude and gestures of kindness
can refuel my heart center with enough caring to
take away the sting of bad news that inures me to

suffering, and I can reclaim my humanity.

Perhaps?

88. The Mathematics of Love

All the signs were there, but he did not
know how to read them and he read them
the wrong way, but it was too much
to bear, and he had to walk away.

Seven long years they were together,
both widows with families of their own,
but it was better to be together than to
be miserable alone.

Then little by little, she began to change;
but for the sake of the relationship, he
forgave her odd behavior, and every year
that passed was worse than the last.

The mathematics of love adds up to disaster
when the mind begins to go, and all the
love in the world cannot erase the damage
that forgetting can do.

89. All the Thorns and Thistles

Man is condemned to be free, said
the ugly little man with all the egotistical
wisdom of his existential conviction; and
man is what he is not and not what he is,
a useless passion without meaning, he
concluded his philosophical treatise with
a conceit worthy of his Nobel laureate
distinction when he failed to resolve the
paradoxical nature of man's free will
and destined purpose; and the ugly little
man with wonky eyes and greasy hair
led the world down the garden path
where all the thorns and thistles choke
out the celestial dream of man's deepest
desire to be what he is meant to be.

90. The Homeless Mind

It's a lonely mind, the homeless mind,
forever in search of meaning, never knowing
what tomorrow will bring.

It's a fearful mind, the homeless mind,
always dreading the end of the day that
cannot promise a new tomorrow.

It's a hopeless mind, the homeless mind
that cannot find a way to resolve
the fear of dying.

And it's an angry mind, the homeless mind,
that murders the image of God like the
mad philosopher Nietzsche.

91. I Have Lived the Life

I have lived the life of an atom in the Body
of God, an embryonic soul with consciousness
but no reflective self-consciousness;

And I have lived the life of a higher primate,
with a power grunt that granted me alpha
status and garnered me self-reflection;

And I have lived the life of a Roman gladiator,
my name was Glaucas, and I was feared
with respect beyond terror;

And I have lived the life of a privileged Roman
nobleman, but I fell in love with a servant woman
with whom I share my life today;

And I have lived the life of an ancient Greek
statesman, my name was Phaedrus, and I was a
student of the philosopher Pythagoras;

And I have lived the life of a North American
Indian, my name was Bear Claw, and I
became the chief of my village;

And I have lived the life of Solomon, a black slave
in the state of Georgia, and when I got caught
for running away, I was whipped to death;

And I have lived the life of a Cockney fishmonger,
pushing my cart through the streets of London,
shouting "Kippers! Fillets!" for my living;

And I have lived the life of a mendicant Sufi in

Medieval Persia, living the secret way, but my love
for God and sexual pleasure drove me insane;

And I have lived the life of debauchery in Paris, France,
and I turned on God, Jesus, and the Holy Mother
Church, and I died in pitiless disgrace;

And I have lived the life of a textile merchant in
Genoa, Italy, Don Giovanni was my name, and I broke
my wife's heart, who is my partner today;

And I have lived the life of an aristocrat in London,
the Earl of Wellington Manor, but I sailed to the new
land of the Americas and become a fur trapper;

And I have lived the life of the man I am today in a
parallel world, returning to my same life again
to achieve a different outcome;

And I have lived the life of a precocious writer
in a future life, and of all the lives that I have lived,
my current lifetime has been the hardest.

92. I Want More, and I Want It Fast

"I want more, and I want it fast,"
said the lady of the land, the fourth
child of an alcoholic and broken
man taken from his home when he
was only ten to be assimilated into
the culture, language, and strange
ways of the people that appropriated
the land from his people and made it
their own; but the times have changed,
as has the moral imperative, and the
people of the land demand their old
ways back, their culture, language,
and much more, and the lady of the
land cried the R-word like a wailing
banshee. *"I want more, and I want
it fast,"* she kept repeating over and
over and over again, like a ghost
hungering for its lost soul.

93. A Pair of Tangled Eagles

Visiting my new friends Bob and Ellen
in my dream, beautiful home, beautiful
couple, good, decent people, twice married
with their own children, grandchildren,
when two dear old friends also dropped by
for a visit. I take my leave for Bob and Ellen
to enjoy their friends, tying my scrubby
old pair of work shoes with frayed laces,
and I look up into the sky and see a flock
of birds flying. My new friends look up too,
and high above the flock of birds, we spot
an eagle soaring with majestic ease, proud
and free; and we spot another eagle soaring
on its own air current, also proud and free;
and they court and tangle, their powerful
talons gripping each other with equal force,
round and round in the big blue sky, they
cartwheel and descend, locked in a spiral
of territorial passion, foretelling, as dreams
often do, the life of my new friends, and
I woke up from my dream with a deeper
understanding of their solid marriage,
and tangled relationship.

94. The God Instinct

I have it, you have it, we all have it,
the God instinct, the need to save each
other from whatever; and try as we
may, we cannot help ourselves. But do
we have to save each other, given that
the world will go on without us? But
the God instinct is too strong, and we
argue just to make our point. Back
and forth we argue, some days louder
and some days softer, like a primordial
need to control; and not until we temper
the God instinct, will we stop trying
to win each other over.

95. Emerson's Poem

One day I met a man who came
from a place of knowing, a land
so far away no one could find it;
and when he spoke, his words
rang so true I believed him. But
who was this man, this stranger
from a strange land, and where
did he get his wisdom? And then
one day, I asked him. He paused,
smiled, and recited Emerson's
poem, *"Gnothi Seauton."*

96. A River of Joy

I caught a faint scent one day,
don't ask me how, but it must
have come from a place so deep
it had to be the scent of God;
and like the Hound of Heaven
in Francis Thompson's poem,
I searched every corner of the
world—North, South, East,
and West—chasing the scent
to the darkest corner of my soul;
but still, I could not find what
I was looking for. But so strong
was the scent of God, it brought
me to Heaven's Door, which
would not open without the key
to my lost soul; so, I surrendered
the love most precious to me, and
I cried inconsolably. But when
Heaven's Door opened wider, I
saw my image in the Face of God,
and I wept a river of joy.

97. Life Goes on As Usual

There's a kind of life that everybody lives,
but nobody knows why, a recurring loop
of everyday living that falls in upon itself
until it blocks out the light; and the darker
it gets, the more we forget how to live
the life we once loved. That's where ennui
comes from, the disease that rots the brain
and kills the soul. But to break this nasty
loop that spawns ennui takes courage;
and, life goes on as usual.

98. The Saddest Spirit of All

When or how it won her over, no
one can be sure, but she conceded
to the saddest spirt of all when she
crossed the line and became one
of the faceless good, and she went
about her way as though nothing
happened; but she knew, and when
*(it could be anything, a movie, poem,
or fleeting memory)* her shame rose
to the nostrils of her conscience, her
betrayed heart bled once more her
precious life-blood as propriety,
the saddest spirit of all, strangled
her thoughtful, caring soul.

99. Ploughing My Way Through Life

Bent over the kitchen sink with my left
elbow resting on the edge of the counter
and my chin in my hand, listening to
the water drip through the Folgers Classic
Roast coffee grounds in the nylon mesh
filter, splashing into the Pyrex coffee pot,
memories of my life flashed through my
mind, and I felt regret for all the times I
ploughed my way through life without
thinking; and then something St. Padre
Pio said to me when he was channeled by
a gifted medium for the novel I wrote
on my spiritual healing came to me, that I
needed those experiences to be where I am
today. But that did not take away the sting
of my stupidity for ploughing my way
through life without thinking, because who
knows where I might be today had I been
more thoughtful; but I can't know for sure
unless I live my life over, which I've done
already to achieve a different outcome that
is my life today. There was enough coffee
in the pot, and I poured a cup to start my day
typing up the story I wrote on my marriage
proposal to the love of my life on her fiftieth
birthday in Duluth, Minnesota. And now
that I reflect on our love, I'm glad I ploughed
my way through life the way I did, because
it brought me to the love I needed to fill the
hole in my soul and justify my impulsive
nature to plough my way through life
without thinking.

100. The Devil's Hindquarter

The devil plays his cards close to his chest,
but not too close, to keep everyone in the
game; and when the devil lays down his
hand, some are surprised and some not,
it all depends upon how well they read
the devil's hand. But all the same, the
devil wins every game, because whoever
plays the devil's game can never get enough
of the devil's hindquarter and wants more,
and they play and play and play until they
beat the devil at his own game and walk
away, free to play their own devil's game,
like writing poetry, holding their cards close
to their chest; but not too close, to keep
the devil wanting more.

Spiritual Musing: "Bee after Bee and the Secret Way"

"Watch the synchronicities, the coincidences,
because they will bring you goodness,"
—St. Padre Pio

I love coincidences. I never know when they will happen, nor does anyone else for that matter *(they have a mind of their own);* but when they happen, they do so for a reason. And one happened the other morning to give me confirmation for something that I already knew, but not quite as gnostically as I would liked to have known; hence, the remarkable little coincidence that confirmed through personal experience what I already knew in my mind. And as confusing as this may seem, this is the inspiration for today's spiritual musing on what Carl Gustav Jung called *"the way of what is to come,"* which he also called the secret way...

In all honesty, when I'm called to write a spiritual musing I never know where my inner guiding principle wants to take me; and no sooner did I write the first paragraph of this spiritual musing, and I caught a glimpse of what I had been called upon to explore—the inexorable mystery of the omniscient guiding principle of the secret way of life that poets have been exploring since forever, what the great American philosopher Ralph Waldo Emerson called "God within."

"Adventure most unto itself /The Soul condemned to be; /Attended by a Single Hound— /Its own Identity," wrote Emerson's contemporary, the mystic poet Emily Dickinson. That's what we're all looking for, our own identity, our true self that the secret way of life points us to through signs, symbols, dreams, coincidences, and especially poetry; which, as I came to see after years of living the secret way of life, can only be found by growing into the person we are meant to be.

That's what made my remarkable little coincidence the other morning so meaningful that it crossed over into the domain of "synchronicity," a word that Jung coined to describe the simultaneous occurrence of events which appear meaningfully related but have no discernable causal connection; hence, meaningful coincidence.

If I may, then. While reading *New York Times* columnist David Brooks' new book the other morning, *The Second Mountain: The Quest for a Moral Life*, I came upon a passage that he believed could very well have been the "pivotal point" of his whole book. He quoted this passage from Annie Dillard's book *Teaching a Stone to Talk*, a collection of her personal meditations:

"In the deeps are the violence and terror of which psychology has warned us. But if you ride these monsters deeper down, if you drop with them farther over the world's rim, you find what our science cannot locate or name, the substrate, the ocean or matrix or ether which buoys the rest, which gives goodness its power for good, and evil its power for evil, the unified field: our complex and inexplicable caring for each other and for our life together here" (*The Second Mountain: The Quest for a Moral Life,* David Brooks, p. 64)

This was my experience also; which, by happy coincidence, I had just explored in my own book *The Fourth Corner of the Abyss* that I was bringing to closure. But because I had never heard of Annie Dillard, whose comment David Brooks felt was pivotal to his new book on his personal quest for a moral life that he had embarked upon five years after writing his book *The Road to Character,* I had to Google the Pulitzer Prize-winning author; and what I found impressed me enough to put two of Annie Dillard's books on my Amazon wish list: *Teaching a Stone to Talk*, and *The Writing Life*—which I *had* to read, because I love reading about what writers have to say about writing. So, I went into Amazon's Look Inside feature and read Chapter One of *The Writing Life* (which she began by quoting Goethe, *"Do not hurry; do not rest,"*), and that's when my remarkable little coincidence happened.

Again, if I may. I was feeling antsy the day before, and it carried over into the morning; and I was antsy because I had been watching too much Netflix, YouTube, and TV to avoid my second reading of Brooks' new book *The Second Mountain*, which I had to read again to refresh my memory and bring my book *The Fourth Corner of the Abyss* to closure with the final chapter "The Five Stages of Life" that a symbolic dream I recently had and Brooks' new book had inspired.

This antsy feeling has happened before, many times in fact, which I've come to define as a mild form of spiritual restlessness that makes me apprehensive, like an annoying itch that cannot be scratched; which was how I was feeling when reading the first chapter of Annie Dillard's book *The Writing Life*.

I had to get myself out of my doldrums, but I didn't really know how—or, I did know how, but I didn't want to slug my way through *The Second Mountain* again, because the second half of the book was mostly padding; and that's when Annie Dillard's name lit up when I read the passage that Brooks had quoted.

So, I Googled her to find out what I could about her, and reading something that she wrote in Chapter One of *The Writing Life* (thanks to Amazon's Look Inside feature) inspired the remarkable little coincidence that gave me the inspiration I needed to get myself out of my doldrums. And here's the passage that did it:

"To find a honey tree, first catch a bee. Catch a bee when its legs are heavy with pollen; then it is ready for home. It is simple enough to catch a bee on a flower: hold a cup or glass above the bee, and when it flies up, cap the cup with a piece of cardboard. Carry the bee to a nearby open spot—best an elevated one—release it, and watch where it goes. Keep your eyes on it as long as you can see it, and hie you to that last known place. Wait there until you see another bee; catch it, release it, and watch. Bee after bee will lead toward the honey tree, until you see the final bee enter the tree. Thoreau describes this process in his journals. So a book leads its writer."

This was not new to me, because I've been a student of the Sufi teaching for years, and Sufis have used this metaphor of bees and honey to pass on the secret teachings of the way *(which flows out of the Sufi poet Rumi in streams of boundless wisdom)*; so, Annie Dillard's passage did not take me by surprise in that sense. It took me by surprise another way, because the timing was perfect—or, meaningfully coincidental, if you will; and I knew instantly what I had to do to get myself out of my annoying little doldrums: I had to be like the bee and go from flower to flower and collect the sweet nectar that I needed to nourish my soul and grow out of my self-inflicted oppressive mood of apprehension *(which I knew would morph into despair if I didn't do something about it)* that took the joy out of my day; so, I opened up a book by one of my favorite poets—*Ten Windows: How Great Poems Transform the World*, by the Zen poet Jane Hirshfield, which was the first "blossom" in my "honey" quest to cure my spiritual malaise.

Jane Hirshfield brought to my attention that poetry does our thinking for us, because when a poet writes a poem, they engage what C. G. Jung called our "transcendent function," which he recognized as our superior insight. And when we engage our higher function *("God within")*, we tap into the creative energy of life, which is the Logos and omniscient guiding principle of life that Jung identified as *"supreme meaning,"* and *"the way of what is to come."*

So, I went to Chapter Four of Jane Hirshfield's book, which, coincidentally enough, was titled "Thoreau's Hound: Poetry and the Hidden," and this chapter inspired me to write my poem, *"Una Bella Giornatta,"* which led to more reading, writing, and the sweet nectar of life—

Una Bella Giornatta

I raised my glass of *Bosco Anice Forte*, clicked
Tony's, and said, "To a good day," but I said it in
broken Italian, because I came to Canada when I
was only five and never learned to speak it properly;
in fact, I had forgotten most of my Italian until I met
Tony, my cottage neighbor, who only comes to his
cottage whenever he can get away, which he would
like to do more often because he loves it here in
Georgian Bay where he can do what he loves to do,
which is simply doing something to keep himself
busy, because doing something fills him with the joy
of fulfillment and gives his life purpose and meaning.

Long-since widowed and with another woman *(the first one didn't work out)*, also Italian and a widow but set in her ways and only comes to the cottage when she's in the right mood, leaving Tony to choose between her and his cottage, but I said to him one day, "She's a good woman, Tony; don't screw this one up," and he listened and they're together still, and yesterday he came to the cottage alone because she was tending to her family *(getting things ready for her grandson's birthday)*, but Tony had to tend to his leaves, which I helped him blow and bag *(plus two wheelbarrows of acorn seeds)*, and he made lunch for us, a barbeque which he loves to do, ten blended lamb and prosciutto skewers, two small Black Angus steaks, and two thick pieces of pancetta, seasoning them with his favorite spices, homemade round Calabrese bread, and a nice hunk of Parmesan-like cheese, *(apologizing for no salad)*, and while waiting for the barbeque, we sipped our *Anice* to warm up from our morning work, and I never felt so good for returning a favor to my good neighbor who has always been there for me. *"Una bella giornatta,"* he said, toasting our friendship when we sat down for lunch at the kitchen table with a glass of his homemade wine.

That's how I "worked" my way out of my annoying little doldrums, by tapping into the creative well of my higher self, which we all have access to if we make the effort. But the trick is to DO something, because doing has the power to send those nasty little demons of depression back to hell where they come from, especially if it is doing for another, as I did in *"Una Bella Giornatta."* Hence revealing the mystery of the Zen koan that I resolved in another poem that I was inspired to write—

Chop Wood, Carry Water

"Before enlightenment; chop wood, carry water.

114

After enlightenment; chop wood, carry water,"
says the Zen koan. But if life, as all indications
would suggest, is a journey to its own destination,
*(1 plus 2 equals 3, and the acorn seed becomes
an oak tree),* then "after enlightenment" would
suggest that one has made the journey to one's
destined purpose and lives life as before the
journey, only now one is enlightened of their
destined purpose; that's the presumption of this
koan, because one has to be enlightened to know
this. And, if life's purpose is to become itself,
what is this "itself" that this koan fails to articulate?
That's the irony of the journey to one's true self
*(whether chopping wood and carrying water,
or working at McDonald's);* and the mystery of
this puzzling koan is revealed: the more we *do*
life, the more *enlightened* we will be.

That's the mystery of *"the way of what is to come,"* the om-
niscient guiding principle of life that fosters resolution through signs,
symbols, dreams, meaningful coincidences, and the redemptive power
of poetry that collects the sweet nectar of life that nourishes our soul's
longing for wholeness and completeness; which, ironically, was the
theme of Brooks' new book, *The Second Mountain: The Quest for a
Moral Life*—proof positive of the secret way of life exemplified by
the author's own quest for self-redemption. And when I finished
reading his book for the second time, I brought my own book *The
Fourth Corner of the Abyss* to happy resolution, and all thanks to one
remarkable little coincidence that opened the door to *"the way of what
is to come"* by way of Annie Dillard's bee after bee analogy.

———

About the Author

Born with a spiritual restlessness that could not be tamed by my Christian faith, I became a spiritual seeker when I discovered reincarnation in Plato's Dialogues at the age of fifteen. I grew up in a small town in Northwestern Ontario, and at twenty-one I had my own pool hall and vending machine business, but my restless spirit called me away to seek out my destiny, and I sold my business and sailed to France.

In the Alpine city of Annecy, in the Haute-Savoie region of France I had a dream that called me to my destiny. I entered into the mind of every person in the world and took every question they had ever asked and reduced them all to one question: *Why am I?* I returned to Canada and went to university to study philosophy to seek an answer to this haunting question, and by "chance" I discovered Gurdjieff, the redoubtable teacher of a system of transformative thought that he called "the Work." His Teaching excited my restless spirit and compelled me to seek out the answer to man's disquieting question in the fast, often tumultuous currents of daily living.

Visit him at: http://ostocco.wix.com/ostocco
http://www.spiritualmusingsbyoreststocco.blogspot.com

ALSO BY OREST STOCCO

POETRY

Not My Circus, Not My Monkeys

NOVELS

The Golden Seed
Tea with Grace
Jesus Wears Dockers
Healing with Padre Pio
Keeper of the Flame
My Unborn Child
On the Wings of Habitat
What Would I Say Today If I Were to Die Tomorrow?

NON-FICTION
The Fourth Corner of the Abyss
One Rule to Live By: Be Good
A Sign of Things to Come
My Writing Life
Death, the Final Frontier
The Merciful Law of Divine Synchronicity
Gurdjieff Was Wrong But His Teaching Works
The Man of God Walks Alone
The Summoning of Noman
The Lion that Swallowed Hemingway
The Sum of All Spiritual Paths
Do We Have An Immortal Soul?
Stupidity Is Not a Gift of God
Letters to Padre Pio
Old Whore Life
Just Going with the Flow
Why Bother? The Riddle of the Good Samaritan
The Pearl of Great Price
In The Shade of the Maple Tree